218 ANIMALS IN FULL COLOR

MAMMALS

A GUIDE TO FAMILIAR AMERICAN SPECIES
a Golden Guide® from St. Martin's Press

by
HERBERT S. ZIM, Ph.D.
and
DONALD F. HOFFMEISTER, Ph.D.
Director, Emeritus, Museum of Natural History,
and Professor, Emeritus, of Ecology,
Ethology, and Evolution,
University of Illinois

Illustrated by
JAMES GORDON IRVING

St. Martin's Press ≈ New York

FOREWORD

MAMMALS is a natural and integral part of the Golden Guide series. Among mammals are animals that man considers the most important animals alive today. Not only do mammals have great economic value, but we enjoy many of them as pets. We thrill at seeing deer alert at the forest edge, and smile at the dignified procession of a mother skunk and her young. Mammals add greatly to the interest of forest, field, and desert.

This volume is a cooperative effort of author, expert, artist, and publisher. Many individuals and institutions have given us their unstinting help in providing advice and information as to text and illustrations, and specimens for the artist. We wish to thank especially the late Edwin Banks, George Batzli, Daniel B. Beard, James Bee, W. H. Burt, the late T. Donald Carter, Wayne Davis, Dean Fisher, Woodrow Goodpaster, the late George G. Goodwin, the late E. R. Hall, David H. Johnson, the late Remington Kellogg, Keith Kelson, William Lidicker, Robert M. McClung, Charles McLaughlin, Karl Maslowski, Joseph C. Moore, Russell Mumford, Ralph Palmer, Charles Potter, Victor Scheffer, the late L. L. Steimley, the late Tracy Storer, the late Hobart Van Deusen, Richard Van Gelder, the late Ralph M. Wetzel, and Ford Wilke.

H.S.Z.
D.F.H.

This is a book for everyone who wants to identify, understand, and enjoy the field mouse scampering through the leaf mold and the squirrel on the branch overhead. Technical details, such as descriptions of skulls, are omitted, and identification is kept at the species level. This book covers 218 of the 350 species of mammals found in the United States and adjacent Canada. The colored plates accent features which help you to recognize the animal in its natural environment.

First become familiar with the mammals pictured and described. Look through the Key to Mammals on the next pages so that you can recognize the major mammal groups. Try to see the mammal well enough to decide, for example, whether it is a rodent or a shrew. Once you place your specimen within a group, thumbing through a few pages will show you the animal or one very much like it. For more detailed identification, use scientific names (pp. 155–156).

Take this book with you on walks and trips. Look up mammals while your impression is fresh. Watch for characteristics that are important in identification. Learn to look carefully. Your first glance may be all you will get. Lengths given in the text are the overall length of the male (including tail), unless otherwise stated. The maps show ranges. If a map shows more than one range, different colors or line patterns are used. The caption within, or nearest to, a certain color or line pattern is the caption that applies to it. In the sample here, red shows the range of Brush Rabbit; blue lines, Desert Cottontail; yellow, Eastern Cottontail. Some maps show present and past ranges.

A KEY TO THE MAMMALS

Here are the major groups (orders and families) into which the mammals you see can be placed:

OPOSSUM: pouch for young, thumb-like big toe, prehensile tail **page 17**

MOLES: burrowers; broad hands, velvety fur, and no external ears **18**

SHREWS: mouse-like; soft fur, long snout, five toes on each foot **21**

BATS: the only flying, winged mammals **25**

CARNIVORES: flesh-eaters; large canine teeth, five toes on front feet **32-65**

Bears: flat-footed, "tail-less"; short, round ears **34**

Raccoons: ring-tailed; black mask (includes Ringtail, Coati) **36**

Weasel Family: short-legged, short-eared; having glands with strong scent. **38**

Foxes, Wolves: dog-like; claws not retractile **52**

Cats: claws retractile; short face and rounded ears **58**

Seals: limbs are flippers **63**

4

RODENTS: Gnawers; only one pair of upper incisor teeth

 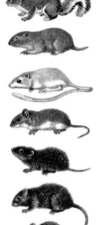
For Beaver, Porcupine, Nutria, Manatee, Armadillo, and a few other mammals not in the above groups, see Index.

Mule Deer fawn

Seeing mammals isn't as easy as seeing birds or flowers. Mammals keep out of sight. Some have concealing colors; some burrow; many are nocturnal. Yet they can be seen if you are patient, alert, and know where to look. Much about mammals is known, but much more remains to be discovered.

WHAT ARE MAMMALS? The name "mammal" refers to the female's mammary glands, which provide milk for her young. This characteristic sets off mammals among the warm-blooded, back-boned animals. Mammals are hairy; young are born alive. Most have varied teeth, for cutting, tearing, or grinding. The mammal's skull is unique; the brain more complex than in other animals.

HOW MANY ARE THERE? There are, the world over, about 15,000 kinds of mammals. Some 3,600 species and subspecies are found in North America. Species number about 650 in North America, 350 north of Mexico. Some are rare, others so common that scores may occur on a single acre.

WHERE ARE THEY FOUND? Mammals live on every continent—in mountains, deserts, arctic snows, marshes, meadows, forests, farms, cities, and the depths of the sea. Some have become adapted to specific environments; thus tree squirrels live only in forests, rice rats only in swamps. More adaptable mammals fit into a variety of environments; thus some rabbits live in woods, some in swamps, some in deserts.

RANGE IN SIZE Mammals range from the Pygmy Shrew to the Blue Whale. Large species, as some carnivores and hoofed mammals, are most familiar. Smaller ones are more common and, in the long run, more important. The larger the mammal, the more land needed to support it. Protecting mammals till their population exceeds the number that a given region will support may mean starvation for the surplus. This happened with deer and elk until hunters were allowed to keep the herds down.

ADAPTATIONS Mammals have developed effective ways of living. One is to care for the young inside the mother before birth. Tooth adaptations vary from the tusks of the peccary to the gnawing teeth of rodents. Feet with hoofs or padded toes are adapted for running, claws for digging, grasping, and climbing, and webs for swimming. Mammals can fly, glide, run, jump, crawl, swim, burrow, and dive. Internal organs show great adaptation, too. Some mammals can hibernate. Such adaptations have made mammals dominant today.

MAMMALS AND MAN Man, most adaptable of mammals, has domesticated and developed others he has needed. Dogs, cats, horses, cattle, sheep, and a score more have been domesticated. Most of these have been improved for human ends. A Holstein cow gives more milk than her ancestors. Those which did not fit our pattern, like the bison and the mountain lion, have suffered badly.

Bison and Holstein Cow

7

ECONOMIC VALUES Mammals helped make America. Pioneers depended on game for everyday food. The fur trade stimulated exploration and settlement. Some mammals are still taken for their furs. Hunting is more than a sport: on the business side, millions are spent yearly for equipment and supplies. Smaller mammals have less obvious values, but provide food for fur-bearers and other predators; many cultivate the soil. Some mammals carry diseases and contaminate foods. All species are so interrelated that each has a role in keeping the natural machinery in balance.

CONSERVATION Our wild mammals are a natural resource, which should be used wisely for the long-range benefit of all the people. National Parks provide complete protection for all wildlife, and here field trips can be most rewarding. State game refuges and those of the U.S. Fish and Wildlife Service protect threatened species such as bison, pronghorn, and elk. National forests are a reservoir of game and smaller animals. Even farms and woodlots can maintain a mammal population. When hunting and trapping are limited to removal of surplus animals, a future supply is assured. You obey hunting and conservation laws because they benefit you, your neighbors, and the country at large.

STUDYING MAMMALS

Identification is the key to exciting hobbies. Once you have begun to study mammals, many possibilities open up.

OBSERVING MAMMALS means more than identification. See how they live, feed, protect themselves, and raise their young. This requires patience. Early or late, your time schedule must fit your subject. Binoculars are an essential. So are warm, comfortable clothes, a notebook, and sometimes a blind or camouflaged shelter. Most economic species have been studied by professional zoologists. Many smaller and less important species still need attention. Experienced amateurs, noting detailed observations, can make a zoological contribution by recording facts on feeding habits, burrows, runways, nests, calls, and behavior of local mammals.

PHOTOGRAPHING MAMMALS can augment your observations. Learn to know your camera first and the habits of your subjects next. Attempt simple, easy subjects first. Light is often poor, so a good lens or flash equipment is important. Animal photography cannot be rushed. Food and water bait often help. Learn to set up your camera so that mammals will take their own pictures.

UNDERSTANDING TRACKS Mammals leave tracks in soft earth, mud, or snow. Many of the tracks will enable you to identify the species without seeing the animal, and tell you the speed and direction the animal was traveling. To better learn to recognize tracks, casts can be made

Select a clear track. Surround by tin can or band. Spread plaster evenly.

of these by pouring a thick solution of plaster of Paris and water over the imprint. When the plaster is dry, lift off the cast; then clean and label it.

MAMMALS AND COMMUNITIES Assemblages of animals and plants with similar environmental requirements can be grouped together in communities. The nature of the vegetation, substrate, climate, and many other factors all interact to affect the kinds of animals that can live in a community. Some communities in the United States with a characteristic mammal include desert (kangaroo rats), grassland-prairie (thirteen-lined ground squirrel), deciduous forest (eastern chipmunk), coniferous forest (red squirrel), and arctic alpine (pikas).

ECOLOGICAL NICHE Just as one mammal differs from another closely related species in certain skeletal or color differences, it also differs in occupying a distinctive habitat as well as distinctive feeding, breeding, and behavioral characters. Collectively, this makes up the ecological niche a given species occupies.

POPULATIONS The number of animals of a given species is dependent upon the quality of the habitat where it lives and the rate that new animals are added, as through births, or removed, as by deaths. Usually there is a balance between the numbers added and removed. However, the balance may be disrupted for a variety of reasons, and the species may be nearly exterminated or become overly abundant. Some species increase in numbers markedly with certain regularity and then have a distinct die-off. These are referred to as cycles and are noticeable in lemmings and voles.

HOME RANGES are established by most mammals much as with birds and other animals. One mammal may occupy a specific area for feeding, rearing young, courting, and resting, more or less to the exclusion of other individuals of the same species. Many species will vigorously defend this range. The size of the home range may differ in summer and winter, and for males and females.

MYTHS A variety of untrue stories about mammals persist. Lemmings do not migrate to the sea and commit suicide although Norwegian lemmings may undergo mass movements that proceed helter-skelter. Bats do not get in one's hair although in cramped quarters their sonar system may become confused and they may nearly fly into a person. Young opossums do not hang from their mother's tail. Porcupines do not shoot their spines, but these will fall out when the animals are shedding hair. Bears do not truly hibernate.

MUSEUMS AND ZOOS are fine places to study. Use them to supplement your field work. A list of well-known museums and zoos is given on p. 154, as well as a list of books for further study.

11

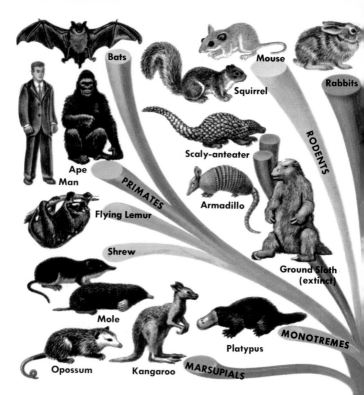

Bats

Mouse

Squirrel

Rabbits

RODENTS

Scaly-anteater

Ape
Man

PRIMATES

Armadillo

Flying Lemur

Ground Sloth
(extinct)

Shrew

Mole

Platypus

MONOTREMES

Opossum

Kangaroo

MARSUPIALS

MAMMALS OF TODAY are probably descended from small- to medium-sized, active, flesh-eating reptiles—the Cynodonts. These reptiles, with mammal-like skulls, bones, and teeth, lived millions of years before the dinosaurs. The first true mammals developed about 190 million years ago, but for over 100 million years they remained an unimportant group of animals. When the dinosaurs died out 70 million years ago, mammals came into their own. By 50 million years ago, three main groups of mammals and most of their subgroups were

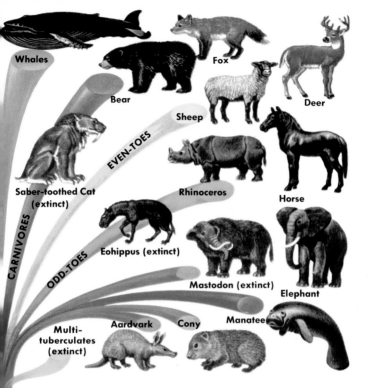

Whales

Bear

Fox

Deer

Sheep

Saber-toothed Cat
(extinct)

EVEN-TOES

Rhinoceros

Horse

CARNIVORES

ODD-TOES

Eohippus (extinct)

Mastodon (extinct)

Elephant

Multi-
tuberculates
(extinct)

Aardvark

Cony

Manatee

well established. The egg-laying mammals, like the Duck-bill and Echidna, are now a small, almost extinct group. The pouched marsupials, whose young are born incompletely developed, are represented by only one species in the United States—the Opossum. All other mammals fit into the great placental group regarded as about 16 living orders. General relationships of the principal orders are shown above. More detailed "trees" are appropriately placed in the book. Study them and become familiar with more detailed relationships.

1. Long-horned Bison

2. Saber-toothed Cat

3. Short-legged Rhinoceros

MAMMALS OF YESTERDAY include some which lived in North America and have become extinct in the past 50 million years. At intervals land bridges from Asia formed, and new mammals came over to compete with and sometimes replace existing species. The Short-legged

14

1. **American Mastodon**

2. **Giant Ground Sloth**

3. **Early Camel**

Rhinoceros lived about 10 million years ago. It became extinct soon after, but other species persisted in Europe till the ice age. The early camel (Procamelus) died out about the same time, but others lived here till the last ice age. More is told about these animals on the next page.

THE FIRST MAMMALS appeared in North America over 75 million years ago. New kinds developed; others came from Asia. About 25 million years later, mammals began to dominate the continent. Many ancient mammals died off, leaving no descendants. Others were ancestors of modern horses, camels, deer, beaver, bison, and rhinos—to mention a few. Smaller mammals were abundant too; their fossils are rarer. Species that have become extinct recently include:

Long-horned Bison was one of a number of species of bison widespread in North America during the ice age. Spear points found with bones of extinct bison show that man hunted them.

Saber-toothed Cats, also found in Europe, were larger in North America. Our species, with dagger-like teeth 8 inches long, survived until late in the ice age.

Short-legged Rhinoceros and kin, developed in North America, became extinct before the ice age. Some migrated to Asia and Africa, where descendants still live.

American Mastodon was one of our many elephant-like animals. Some had shovel-tusks; some, curved pointed tusks. The Woolly Mammoths, surviving into the ice age, were hunted by early man, perhaps Indians.

Giant Ground Sloth was an elephant-sized member of a group which today has few members. Heavy hind legs and tail suggest it squatted when feeding or resting. It was contemporary with early man in North America.

Early Camel (Procamelus) represents the midpoint in the development of the camel in North America. From here, types of camels moved into Asia and South America, where they live today. Other, larger kinds of camels survived here into the ice age.

OPOSSUM is our only native marsupial or pouched mammal. Baby opossums, which weigh only 1/15 oz. at birth, live in the mother's fur-lined pouch about 3 months. Up to 14 may be born; usually only 7 to 9 survive. Opossums hunt at night for small birds and mammals. They eat eggs and fruit also. When threatened by enemies, they "play possum" and collapse as if dead. Opossums are recognized by their white faces, coarse fur, and rat-like tails. Males and females are alike. *Length:* 33 in.

Newborn Opossums

1. Star-nosed Mole

2. Hairy-
tailed
Mole

MOLES are small, plump, underground creatures, with velvety fur, no visible ears, and eyes reduced or absent. They have powerful shoulders, a short neck, muscular front legs with shovel-like feet, and heavy claws—all features useful in digging. Sensitive snouts and sensory

hair on front feet and tail keep moles from bumping into tunnel walls. Distinguish the Hairy-tailed Mole by its hairy tail and short snout. Star-nosed Mole is identified by an odd, pink, disc-like fringe on its snout.

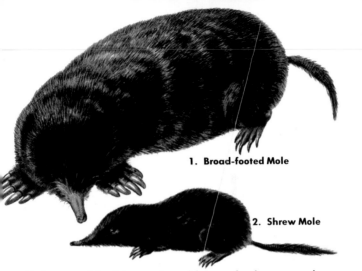

1. Broad-footed Mole

2. Shrew Mole

Moles tunnel in rich woods and lawns, feeding on grubs and worms. The Broad-footed Mole, one of several western species, is almost blind. It resembles the Eastern Mole (p. 20), but with a more fleshy tail. The Shrew Mole has a long snout and hairy tail. The smallest mole (5 in.), it spends more time at the surface than others. In many features, it is intermediate between moles and shrews. Other moles range from 5½ to 8 in. long.

MOLE SNOUTS

Star-nosed

Shrew

Shrew
Mole

Broad-footed
Mole

19

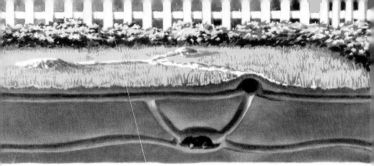

Mole hills and tunnels

THE EASTERN MOLE or common mole makes the mounds that dot your lawn. You are unlikely to see any moles, for they stay underground unless molested. Moles

dig two types of tunnels: deep tunnels (to 2 ft. underground) where they nest, spend the winter, and remain during drought; and shallow tunnels seen on lawns, along which they find insects and earthworms. *Length:* 7 in.

PYGMY SHREWS are the smallest shrews, and shrews, in general, are the smallest North American mammals. The Pygmy Shrew weighs only 1/14 ounce—less than a dime. As it darts through dry woods and clearings, where it lives, people mistake it for a mouse. Note its velvety, soft, mole-like fur, slender body and legs, and short tail. Shrews feed on small insects, which they hunt constantly. Because of their activity and small size, they consume several times their weight in food every day. Shrews spend more time above ground than moles. Their eyesight is better, too. Enemies: common carnivores, owls, hawks, snakes. *Length*: about 3 in.

21

(Text on page 24.)

1. Arctic Shrew

2. Masked Shrew

3. Least Shrew

Arctic

Masked

Least

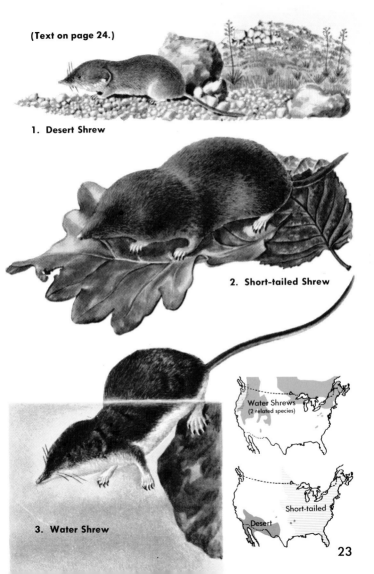

(Text on page 24.)

1. Desert Shrew

2. Short-tailed Shrew

3. Water Shrew

Water Shrews
(2 related species)

Short-tailed

Desert

23

Pygmy Shrew

SHREWS, our smallest but fiercest mammals, attack and kill prey several times their weight. Two shrews may fight till one kills and consumes the other. The young (four to five), born in a hollow stump, log, or burrow, can fend for themselves within a month. The life span is short—one and a half years at most.

Masked Shrew is a common, widespread, long-tailed shrew, found in moist forest localities. *Length: 4 in.*

Arctic Shrew is similar to Masked Shrew, but larger, with a longer tail. Its coat is brown above, gray-white below, changing in winter to a darker brown or blackish above and almost white below. *Length: 4½ in.*

Least Shrew, small and short-tailed, inhabits grassy abandoned fields. Feeds on insects, possibly mice.

Desert Shrew, pale, ashy-gray in color, lives amid cacti and sagebrush in more arid places than any other of our shrews. Not often found. *Length: 3 in.*

Short-tailed Shrew, with stubby tail, is one of the commonest mammals of eastern woods. Its slightly poisonous saliva aids in paralyzing prey. *Length: 4½ in.*

Water Shrews can run on water, with their large, broad, hairy feet. They also swim and dive, feeding under water on insects, fish, and fish eggs. *Length: 6 in.* Northern Water Shrew is more black; the Pacific species is more brown.

1. Long-nosed Bat   2. Leaf-nosed Bat   3. Mastiff Bat

BATS are the only flying mammals. Flying squirrels glide, but only bats fly. Bats' forelimbs are greatly modified and form wings very different from those of birds. In bats, the fingers are greatly lengthened to support a thin membrane. This membrane extends to the hind legs. The legs and usually the tail support the membrane.

Bats have limited eyesight. In flight their large ears form part of a unique system for locating and avoiding objects. Bats emit a sound, too high-pitched for us to hear, which is echoed back like a radar beam. Picked up by the bat's sensitive ears, this echo indicates the direction and distance of obstacles to be avoided and of flying insects that may be seized for food.

About 2,000 kinds of bats inhabit temperate and tropical regions. The 65 or so kinds found in the United States are primarily insect-eaters. Some larger, tropical bats feed on fruit, and the Vampire Bats of South and Central America feed on blood. Long-nosed Bats feed on pollen of night-blooming flowers. Bats rest during the day, hanging upside down in caves, in deserted buildings, under cliffs, and in trees. At dusk they fly out to feed on insects. Their erratic flight and the darkness make identification difficult. For positive identification, find some at rest during the day. Catch them in barns, under cliffs and in caves. Release them after you have studied them.

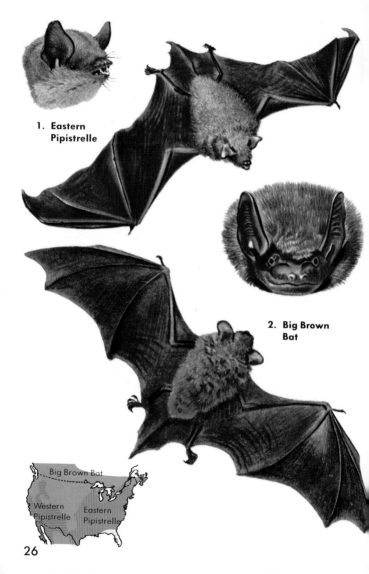

1. Eastern
   Pipistrelle

2. Big Brown
   Bat

Big Brown Bat

Western
Pipistrelle

Eastern
Pipistrelle

26

1. Silver-haired Bat

2. Big-eared Bat

Silver-haired

Big-eared

(Text on page 28.)

PIPISTRELLES are the smallest American bats (*length:* 3 in.). The erratic flight, in early evening, and small size are clues to identification. Eastern Pipistrelle has reddish-brown fur, black at base, and brownish ears. Western Pipistrelle has grayish-brown fur, blackish ears. Both hibernate.

BIG BROWN BATS are large bats (*length:* 4½ in.) often seen around dwellings. Bats that fly in through windows or down chimneys are usually Big Browns, harmless like other bats. Young are born in late spring. They grow rapidly and in two months reach adult size. Rarely live in large colonies, as do Pipistrelles and Little Brown Bats.

SILVER-HAIRED BAT is a dark bat (*length:* 4 in.) with silver-tipped fur, which is more pronounced on the back. They are common, slow-flying bats, often seen along mountain streams and lakes. At rest they are usually solitary, hanging from branches in deep woods or hiding under loose bark of trees. Migrates to the southern part of its range in fall. May be confused with the larger Hoary Bats (p. 31).

BIG-EARED BATS are large (*length:* 4 in.) with ears larger than the head, and two large lumps on top of the nose (also called Lump-nosed Bats). Fur is reddish brown; males and females alike. They frequent caves, coming out at dusk to feed. The eastern species of Big-eared Bat is silvery below; the western Big-eared, brownish below.

Little Brown Bats resting

LITTLE BROWN BATS and their kin are a group of common small bats with long, narrow ears and "simple" faces. Over a dozen species occur in North America, most about 3½ in. long. A single young is born in early summer and can fly in a few weeks. The bats may make several feeding flights a night in search of small flying insects. When cold weather sets in, these bats hibernate. Thousands have been found in larger caves— sometimes in clusters, sometimes forming a layer over the cave walls. They also live in deserted buildings.

American Free-tailed Bats

PALLID and AMERICAN FREE-TAILED BATS are large western species. The Pallid, one of our palest bats, is larger (*length*: 4½ in.) and drab gray in color. It has very large ears, ridged nose without lumps, and broad wings. Often found near buildings, these bats fly slowly and feed close to the ground. Free-tailed Bats have nearly half the tail projecting beyond the membrane. Their musk glands produce a disagreeable odor. Millions of these American Free-tails live in the upper parts of Carlsbad Caverns in New Mexico.

1. American Free-tailed Bat

2. Pallid Bat

Pallid and relatives

American Free-tailed

RED and HOARY BATS are widespread species, but the former is more common. The Red Bat (*length:* 4½ in.) is easily recognized by its rusty-red fur, tipped with white. Females are duller—an unusual condition, since both sexes in bats generally look alike. These bats migrate south in fall and spend the winter in warmer latitudes. The Hoary Bat is a large (*length:* 5 in.) forest species. Its brown fur, tipped with white, gives it a silvery appearance. Males usually fly alone, females in small groups. A pair of young, born in midsummer, is carried by the mother as she feeds.

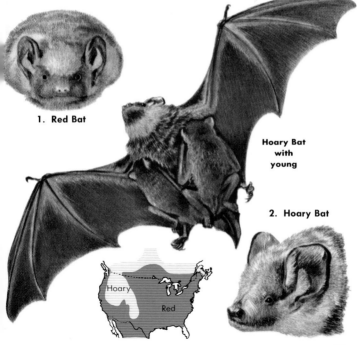

1. Red Bat

Hoary Bat with young

2. Hoary Bat

Hoary

Red

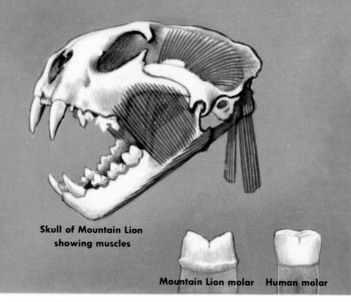

Skull of Mountain Lion
showing muscles

Mountain Lion molar   Human molar

CARNIVORES are a well-known group. Most are predators—quick, intelligent, and sometimes vicious. Many are built for speed—among them the cat family, which includes the fastest mammals. Carnivores show adaptations for hunting. The most obvious are in the mouth. The lower jaw moves freely, for grasping and gripping. Teeth are sharp, for cutting and tearing. The feet of carnivores are padded, some with sharp claws.

Three families of carnivores are aquatic and have webbed feet (seals and walruses, pp. 63-65). Seven familes are

Mountain Lion   Raccoon   Mink

Dogs

Weasels

Foxes

Badgers

Civets

Bears

Hyenas

Raccoons

Cats

Seals

Creodont Carnivores

Shrews   Creodonts   Hoofed Mammals

land animals, although some species (River and Sea Otters) are excellent swimmers, adapted to water life. Carnivores range in size from the tiny Least Weasel to half-ton bears. Some supplement their flesh diet with fish. A few eat fruits and berries. As predators, the carnivores help in keeping the population of rodents and other plant-eaters in check. The group includes some of the best fur bearers (otter, mink, marten, fox, and raccoon). Large numbers of mink and fox are successfully raised on fur farms.

Fox   Otter   Bear

BLACK BEARS, despite their name, vary from brown to black in color, sometimes with white on the chest. Note the bear's unusual flat-footed walk. Young (usually two), born in late winter while the mother is dormant, remain with her till the following fall. Then each seeks a den under a fallen log or rocky ledge for winter sleep. Bears feed on small mammals, fish, plants, and especially on wild berries. *Length:* to 6 ft.; *height:* 3 ft.; *weight:* about 300 lb.

GRIZZLIES (including the Alaskan Brown bears) are so called because the lighter tip of each hair gives their coats a silvery look. They are the largest land carnivores, now protected. Once widespread, a few still occur in the Rockies, Canada, and Alaska. Grizzlies feed on game, berries, and honey, and scoop up salmon as they come up the rivers to spawn. Indians once made necklaces of their claws. *Length:* to 8 ft.

35

RACCOON, identified by black mask and ringed tail, is one of the best-known medium-sized mammals. It feeds on rodents, insects, frogs, wild fruit, and corn, and washes its food when near water. The den is often in a hollow tree. Three to six young, born in spring, are blind for about three weeks. They remain in the den for two months and with parents till the following spring. They are curious and mischievous. *Length:* to 32 in.

1. Ringtail

2. Coati

RINGTAILS and COATIS are both related to raccoons. The former (upper picture) is also called Ring-tailed Cat. The Ringtail (*length:* about 30 in.), with white around the eyes and a longer tail than that of raccoons, feeds on small animals. Coatis have longer noses and long, partly ringed tails. They travel in bands, feeding on insects and on some plants. The mischievous Coatis are more widely distributed in Central and South America. *Length:* 40 to 50 in.

Ringtail

Coati

Fisher

Marten

Mink

Weasel

Black-footed Ferret

Wolverine

River Otter

Hog-nosed Skunk

Striped Skunk

Spotted Skunk

OTTERS

WEASEL-LIKE MAMMALS

SKUNKS

Sea Otter

BADGERS

THE WEASEL FAMILY includes skunks, otters, badgers, and mink—all small- to medium-sized animals with small heads, long tails, sharp teeth, and claws. They are prized fur bearers whose skins bring top market prices. This family occurs in North and South America, Europe, Asia, and Africa. Our species are more common in cooler, wooded regions. True Weasels and Wolverines (p. 45) are aggressive predators. The skunks have a slow, quiet dignity. All members of the family have scent glands, but those of the skunk are most powerful. The ranges of these mammals have shrunk as man has encroached on them.

MARTENS, close relatives of the Fisher (p. 42), are smaller (*length*: 2 ft.) and show more preference for trees. They hunt squirrels, rabbits, and birds. In the hollow-tree nest two to four young are born in spring; by fall they fend for themselves. Martens are sometimes called Sable—the name of a species native to northern Europe and Asia. Marten fur is prized, and some animals have been raised in captivity. Trapping and cutting of northern pine forests have greatly reduced the wild Marten population.

Nest in hollow tree

Short-tailed Weasel in summer and winter

WEASELS, three species of them, are brownish in summer. They have long, shiny hair and soft fur, the undersides and feet being lighter. These slim-bodied, determined hunters often kill more than they can eat. They prey on mice, rats, shrews, and moles, and will attack larger animals: squirrels, rabbits, and poultry. A weasel in a henhouse can be a catastrophe. In turn, weasels are eaten by owls, hawks, cats, and larger members of the weasel family. Weasels are the quickest mammals, their movements being almost too fast to follow, but they are curious and are easily trapped. Weasels use burrows of other animals for a nest, lining it with fur and feathers. In spring, four to eight young are born. In five to seven weeks the young can care for themselves.

Short-tailed Weasel, sometimes called Ermine, is a common northern species. In winter, its pelage turns white, but the tail retains the black tip. In summer a white line runs down inside the hind legs. *Length:* 10½ in.

Long-tailed Weasel is the most common and widely distributed (*length:* about 16 in.). In the Southwest and Florida, it has a whitish band across the face (bridled weasel).

Least Weasel, even shorter (*length:* 6 in.), is the smallest of carnivores. Less common than the others, it lacks the black tip to its tail and is always completely white in winter. It feeds on insects and, in winter, on mice and shrews.

1. **Least Weasel**   2. **Long-tailed Weasel (below)**

FISHER is a big, agile weasel with a heavy, bushy tail and a silky pelt. The fur is very valuable, and so for years Fishers were continually hunted and trapped. Although a good swimmer, the Fisher does not fish. It is a nimble tree-climber and looks above ground for most of its food: small mammals, birds, fruit, and nuts. It is reputed to be the fastest mammal in trees and is nearly

as fast on the ground. Fishers live in moist forests. They store extra food and return to eat it. Young, three to a litter, are born in early spring and begin to hunt in about three months. *Length:* to 3 ft.

MINK live near water. They are aggressive hunters with a special taste for Muskrat, sometimes destroying entire colonies. They also eat fish, other mammals, marsh birds, and poultry. Mink are constantly on the go, carrying their young by the scruff of the neck on land or pickaback in water. When angry, Mink discharge an acrid musk. They spit and squeal with rage. The young (five to six) are the size of pea pods at birth and are covered with fine whitish hairs. Mink fur is valuable. Several varieties are raised in captivity. *Length*: to 20 in.; *weight*: to 2 lb. Female smaller.

Blue Mink

Platinum Mink

43

BLACK-FOOTED FERRET is the largest true weasel (up to 18 in. long, with 6-in. tail). The Blackfoot is light-colored, except for its feet and for a dark band across its eyes. A resident of open plains, it feeds mainly on prairie dogs and ground squirrels. A Ferret will work its way through the burrows of a prairie-dog colony, killing many of them. All weasels have musk glands at the base of the tail, but the Blackfoot has a stronger odor than most. The removal of prairie dogs, by poisoning, has nearly eliminated these Ferrets in many areas. Closely related to the Asian polecats.

Originally

WOLVERINES, brown, and shaggy-haired, are the largest members of the weasel family, reaching 3 ft. in length. They feed on rabbits, gophers, other small mammals, and birds, and are known to kill game as large as deer and elk. Wolverines rob traps and destroy caches of trappers' food. They are powerful, ill-tempered animals. Their range extends south over the U.S. border in the western mountains, but the animal is common in Canadian forests and in Alaska. It builds an underground den lined with leaves. Here three to four young are born each summer.

OTTERS are large, aquatic weasels. Two kinds live in North America—the Sea and the River Otters.

Sea Otter, larger than River Otter, has a most valuable pelt. Adapted for marine life, it has webbed hind feet and soft, heavy fur, said to be the world's best. Sea Otters live along rocky Pacific shores, California to Alaska, feeding on sea urchins, clams, and fish. Rarely going on land, they rest floating on the back, front paws folded on the chest. Once fairly common, they were hunted till nearly extinct. Now protected, they are returning to isolated bays. *Length:* 5 ft.

Sea Otter

River Otter, much more common and widespread, has the reputation of being a fun-loving animal. Otters chase one another, wrestle, tumble, and slide down muddy stream banks. They are excellent swimmers. Otters live on small fish, but also eat muskrats, small mammals, snails, crayfish, insects, frogs, snakes, and some birds. A den is made in the stream bank or in the base of a hollow tree. Here the female has two or three pups in late spring. The young grow slowly and stay with her for nearly a year. During that time, the mother teaches them to swim and hunt. The young play together or with their mother. Otters travel by water but will move overland if necessary. Their fur is warm, remarkably thick, and very durable, rating much higher than mink.

Length: to 4¼ ft.

River Otter

STRIPED SKUNK, with its two white stripes down the back, is a source of endless jokes because it squirts a smelly fluid from scent glands under its tail. However, it gives fair warning before squirting, by stamping forefeet, hissing, and raising its hair. This common skunk lives on forest borders, fence rows, and open meadows. It hunts at night for mice, rats, chipmunks, and all kinds of insects. The young, three to eight, are born blind in a burrow. They grow rapidly. The white stripes may vary in length. *Length:* to 40 in.

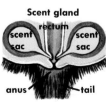

Scent gland

rectum

scent sac

scent sac

anus

tail

48

SPOTTED SKUNK, playful and nimble, has very soft fur. It is the smallest skunk in the U.S., but its scent is as strong as that of larger species. Also called Civet Cat, it lives in waste places, in brush, and under farm buildings. Like other skunks it hunts at night, feeding on insects, small rodents, lizards, snakes, and fruits. Spotted Skunks may warn enemies with a unique handstand—back erect and tail waving. The tiny young (usually four to a litter) are born in early spring. Within five months they are as big as their parents. *Length:* to 22 in.; females slightly smaller.

Striped

Spotted

HOG-NOSED SKUNKS have a naked, hog-like snout and a broad white band from the top of the head over the entire back to the white tail. They grow to about 28 in. Found only in the Southwest, these unusual skunks have come north from Mexico and Central and South America, where they are more common. They dig up lar-

vae, grubs, other insects, and worms; birds, eggs, and berries are also eaten. Hog-nosed Skunks have small litters. They are less common than other skunks; fur, shorter and coarser; claws, heavier and longer.

50

AMERICAN BADGER is a fierce, powerful fighter with few enemies, except the largest carnivores. It can hold its own against a pack of dogs. Note the heavy body; short, bushy tail; white stripe and patches on face; and long claws on forefeet. Badgers burrow and tunnel after small rodents. Sometimes they eat snakes, birds, and birds' eggs. The female builds herself a nest of grass at the end of a deep burrow. Here a litter of three to four young are born during May or June. By fall the young are able to care for themselves. *Length:* over 2 ft., *weight:* to 20 lb.

Badger burrow

THE FOX OR DOG FAMILY comprises widespread, familiar carnivores, found the world over. Most are medium-sized, active, gregarious animals, best described as "dog-like." Different species are similar in general appearance and have not changed markedly through the ages. Fossils of 30-million-year-old "dogs" indicate they were very much like those of today. Dogs have five toes on the front feet and usually four on the rear. Cats can retract their claws; dogs cannot. Some of these flesh eaters also eat fruit and berries. American species include foxes, coyotes, and wolves.

Cynodictis, dog-like mammal of 40 million years ago

KIT FOXES, small, with big ears, are the pygmies of the fox group. They rarely grow as much as a yard long, including a foot of bushy tail. When pursued, they run incredibly fast. Kit Foxes are found in arid, open country. The Great Plains species, known as the Swift, has been greatly reduced. Kit Foxes feed largely on desert rodents, also insects, lizards, and birds. When possible, this Fox carries prey to its den. Here four or five young are born in early spring. Both father and mother help in raising the family.

53

1. Cross Fox   1. Black Fox

RED and GRAY FOXES live over most of the United States. The Red Fox spreads north into Canada and Alaska. Gray Foxes prefer warmer regions. The Gray Fox (*length: 32 to 40 in.*) is slightly smaller than the Red (*length: 36 to 40 in.*). Arctic Foxes, found in both Alaska and Canada, develop white fur in winter, but the fur of Red and Gray Foxes remains unchanged. Both foxes feed on rodents, other small mammals, carrion, poultry, and occasionally fruit and berries. Both prefer open forest and brushland where there is cover for hunting.

1. Red Fox

1. Silver Fox

In the West, Gray Foxes prefer open country. They occasionally climb trees. Foxes build dens in sandy banks. Here about five young are born in late spring. Both parents care for the young and teach them to hunt. By winter the young are ready to care for themselves. The Red Fox has several attractive color forms: Cross, Silver, and Black. All color phases may occur in one litter. Foxes are raised on farms for their fur.

2. Gray Fox

COYOTE looks like an underfed police dog. Despite past efforts to exterminate them, Coyotes have survived, are spreading, and in some places increasing in numbers. Their howling is still a familiar sound. Coyotes are intelligent animals. They eat nearly everything: carrion, rodents, rabbits, some insects, game, poultry, and fruit. The young, born in April, in dens or shallow burrows, stay with parents till fall. *Length:* to 3 ft.

Originally

Now
(extended)

WOLVES were once common in all but the driest parts of this country. They hunted deer, elk, rabbits, and even smaller mammals. As farms were opened, they found settlers' cattle and sheep an easy banquet. Gray or Timber Wolf, now more abundant in Canada and Alaska, grows 5 to 6 ft. long, almost 30 in. high at the shoulder, and weighs 80 to 150 lb. The Red Wolf of the South is smaller.

Gray Wolf Now (red)

Red Wolf Now (yellow)

Gray Wolf

Jaguar

Mountain Lion

Lion

Cheetah

Jaguarundi

Saber-toothed Cat

Lynx

THE CAT FAMILY includes large and small species, but all have a few common characteristics—short faces, blackened, rough tongue, sharp cutting teeth, and padded feet with retracting claws. This family, like the preceding, was once widely distributed. Now all species, and especially the larger cats, are reduced in number and in range. The common domestic cat, a descendant

Libyan Cat

of a Libyan cat tamed by Egyptians centuries ago, now may run wild miles from habitations. Like its wilder relatives, it feeds on rodents, other small mammals, and birds.

MOUNTAIN LIONS, known also as cougars, pumas, or panthers, are, next to jaguars, the largest American cats. They have small heads, long bodies and tails. Color varies from light tan to a tawny brown. Now very rare, these lithe beasts leap on prey from trees or rocky ledges. They kill deer, smaller mammals and sometimes cattle, but normally fear and avoid man. Litters of two to five, born in late winter or early spring, stay with the mother two years. *Length:* to 8 ft.; *weight:* 200 lb.

Now

Originally

LYNX is a handsome, stub-tailed cat with thick, soft fur. It is larger and paler than the Bobcat, to which it is closely related, with longer ear tufts and legs. Its name comes from the Greek and refers to its sharp eyesight or bright eyes. A shy night prowler of northern woods and mountains, it preys on small mammals, particularly

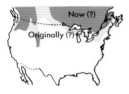

Snowshoe Rabbits, and on birds, snakes, and fowl. Its large feet enable it to walk on the snow when other animals would sink. Young (one to four) are born in late spring in a rock den or hollow tree. *Length:* to 3 ft.

BOBCAT, aptly called Wildcat, is a small, fearless hunter that may attack animals many times its size. It usually feeds on rabbits, ground squirrels, mice, and birds. The Bobcat prefers hunting on the ground, although it can climb trees. It usually hunts within the same area of 4 to 5 sq. mi. of forest, or semi-arid tablelands. It dens in hollow trees or other protected places. Note the bobbed tail. This wary animal is rarely seen. Two to four young are born in late spring and stay with their mother till fall. By the time they are ready to leave, they can hunt. *Length:* to 3 ft.; *weight:* to 25 lb.

Originally

Now (?)

JAGUARS, which look like Old World leopards, include the largest and most powerful American cats. The South American kinds are the largest. Jaguars prefer dense thickets but can live in deserts as well as in wet jungles. Jaguars attack large and small mammals and have no enemies but man. The young (two to four), born in late spring, are more spotted than the adults. They require two years to mature, staying with the mother nearly all that time. *Length:* to 7 ft.; *weight:* to 250 lb. Females smaller.

Originally (?)
Now

FAMILY TREE OF AQUATIC CARNIVORES

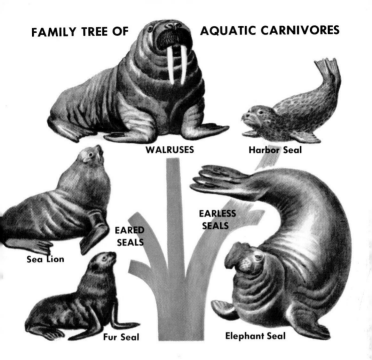

WALRUSES

Harbor Seal

EARLESS SEALS

EARED SEALS

Sea Lion

Fur Seal

Elephant Seal

SEALS and SEA LIONS, together with Walruses, make up the three families of aquatic carnivores. All are grace-ful, powerful swimmers that feed on fish and other marine life. Their legs are modified into flippers; their bodies are streamlined. On land, where seals come to rest and raise their young, they are slow and clumsy. Animals can be slaughtered readily at certain times of the year, and herds need to be protected. Several species, like the Elephant Seal, are still rare and may never stage a comeback. The Fur Seals of the Pribilof Islands, once nearly exterminated, now through wise management number between 1.3 and 1.8 million, with a potential fur value of 3 to 6 million dollars annually.

California Sea Lion

SEA LIONS and their relatives, the Fur Seals, have ears. Other seals are earless. The Northern Sea Lion is a huge beast weighing up to 1,700 lb. The California Sea Lion is smaller (*weight*: to 600 lb., *length*: to 8 ft.) and lives farther south. Males are much larger than females, which have only a single pup at a time. Sometimes both species are seen together, feeding on fish and

 squid. Females of the smaller species may be captured young and trained for circus work, because of their intelligence and fine sense of balance. All circus seals are California Sea Lions.

HARBOR SEALS are small and remain close to land, near harbors, bays, and mouths of rivers. Unlike other seals, Harbor Seals frequently come ashore to rest and sleep. They hunt alone, feeding on fish and crustaceans, but congregate in herds on land. Their enemies are sharks, killer whales, and man. Each fall, these seals grow a new coat of coarse, spotted hair, varying in color from yellowish gray to near-black. The single young or pup is born white but soon sheds and grows a spotted coat. It has to be taught to swim and to catch fish. *Length:* about 5 ft.; *weight:* 150 lb.

1. Beaver, 30 in.

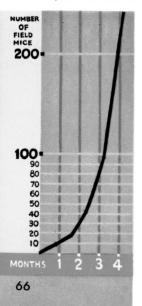

2. Field Mouse, 6 in.

Reproduction potential of a pair of field mice

NUMBER OF FIELD MICE

200
100
90
80
70
60
50
40
30
20
10

MONTHS 1 2 3 4

RODENTS, the largest order of mammals, are the most successful and most widespread group. Rodents are to be found on every continent and all oceanic islands, from the arctic to the tropics, below sea level to above timber line. They greatly outnumber human beings. Those species that travel with man quickly take over new domains. Over 1,600 kinds (subspecies) of rodents are found in North America.

Rodents are generally small; most are less than a foot long and well under a pound in weight. The few exceptions include beavers, which may weigh 50 to 60 lb. Characteristic of rodents are four prominent, yellow or orange incisor teeth. These continue to grow during the entire lifetime of the animal. As these wear, the hard enamel on their surface forms a sharp, chisel-like edge. After these teeth comes a distinct gap in the jaw before the chewing teeth, which never total more than 18. The food of rodents is mainly vegetable; some species eat insects and other animal food.

North American rodents fit into 13 families (8 in U.S.). Our largest families are the squirrels, mainly active by day, and the mouse family, which includes New and Old World mice

New World Rats & Mice

Kangaroo Rats

Pocket Gophers

Voles

Squirrels

Old World Rats & Mice

Jumping Mice

Beavers

Porcupines

Aplodontia

Paramys (primitive rodent)

and rats and various voles. Some rodents dwell underground; some in trees; some are semi-aquatic. Not all rodents are harmful; most have little economic effect. Muskrat, nutria, and beaver have valuable furs. Many rodents provide food for meat-eating mammals. Only a few native rats, mice, and gophers cause damage. Those that do are the more dangerous because they mature rapidly and breed frequently. An acre of land may have 10 to 300 Meadow Mice; the record is nearly 10,000 per acre. Drastic rises and falls of rodent population may occur. Introduced Old World house mice, Norway Rats, and Roof Rats are destructive.

Antelope Squirrels

Mantle Squirrels

Chipmunks

Ground Squirrels

Prairie Dogs

Tree Squirrels

Woodchucks

Flying Squirrels

GROUND
DWELLERS

TREE
DWELLERS

THE SQUIRREL FAMILY is a large and diverse group including ground as well as tree species, and some species—such as woodchucks—which do not look like squirrels at all. Despite these differences, all squirrels have bushy or at least furry tails and fairly rounded heads. Some members of this group are eaten. Squirrel stew was once a standard dish, and woodchucks have graced tables. Nearly all terrestrial squirrels have a long winter sleep—hibernation.

WOODCHUCKS hibernate in deep burrows from early October to February. When they emerge, their shadows do not foretell the weather, despite the superstition. Until gardens and wild plants are up, woodchucks have a hard time getting enough food. Two to six young are born in April. Their eyes open four weeks later. By fall they are nearly full grown, if they have escaped hunters, hawks, foxes, and coyotes. *Length:* to 2 ft.; *weight:* to 12 lb. Females similar to males, but smaller.

69

1. Hoary Marmot

2. Yellow-bellied Marmot

MARMOTS are western relatives of woodchucks and belong to the same genus. Hoary Marmots are found from the Pacific Northwest up through Alaska. Their shrill, whistling call is common in mountains, where they live under loose rocks. *Length:* 25 to 30 in. The Yellow-bellied Marmot is a smaller, social animal of lower slopes of western mountains. Yellowish fur on the abdomen accounts for its name. Marmots are food for coyotes, foxes, wolves, and bobcats.

Hoary and relatives

Yellow-bellied

THIRTEEN-LINED GROUND SQUIRREL, widely distributed on prairie and plain, is 8 to 12 in. long. These "gophers" damage some crops but also eat insects, mice, and small birds. They, in turn, are food for carnivores, hawks, and snakes. After a summer of feeding, they hibernate in a grass-lined chamber at the end of a long tunnel. Here the six to ten young are born about a month after spring mating. They leave the nest when six weeks old. These ground squirrels are gradually extending their range eastward.

1. Richardson Ground Squirrel

2. Townsend Ground Squirrel

3. Franklin Ground Squirrel

4. Spotted Ground Squirrel

Richardson
Spotted

Franklin
Townsend
Antelope

72

GROUND SQUIRRELS are striped or spotted burrowing rodents of several closely related groups. Typical are:

Richardson Ground Squirrel is grayish brown, medium-sized, 10 in. long, with very small ears and a short (2 to 4 in.) tail, which is bordered by white or light gray. They live in colonies in meadows and sagebrush.

Townsend Ground Squirrel is a small (5 to 7 in.), grayish animal with a short tail. Lives in dry sagebrush valleys. Young: seven to ten in a litter.

Franklin Ground Squirrel (*total length:* 14 to 16 in.) is larger and more gray than other plains "gophers." It inhabits prairies, pastures, planted fields. Diet: grass, soft plants, and seeds; some insects and small mammals.

Spotted Ground Squirrel is a pale, spotted species, about 9 in. long. Lives in sandy soil, near rocks, never straying far from its burrow. Its call is a bird-like whistle.

Antelope Ground Squirrel of the Southwest runs with its tail curled over its back. Common in desert areas, they feed mainly on seeds.

Antelope Ground Squirrel

73

GOLDEN-MANTLED GROUND SQUIRREL, a handsome rodent, is more chipmunk-like than its relatives, but has a heavier build and lacks the stripes which chipmunks have on the side of the face. The Golden-mantled Ground Squirrel is easily seen in western pine forests, among rocks and fallen timber. Its reddish head and the white stripe with black borders on each side of its back

are conspicuous. Like other ground squirrels, it digs burrows for shelter, for raising its three to seven young, and for hibernating in winter. Food: seeds, especially pine, and fruit. *Length:* 10 to 11 in.

ROCK GROUND SQUIRRELS, found in the Southwest, are our largest terrestrial squirrels. Rock Squirrels resemble tree squirrels in appearance, with long, bushy tails. They inhabit rocky places, from deserts to mountain tops, nesting and hibernating under stones. Although they often perch on some boulder or vantage point, their dull gray color makes them hard to see. Nuts, seeds, grasses, and grains are preferred foods, though some insects are eaten occasionally. The California Ground Squirrel is similar in appearance and habits. *Length:* 17 to 21 in.

PRAIRIE DOGS are closely related to the ground squirrels (pp. 71–75). They are social animals living in large colonies or "towns" marked by low mounds of bare dirt and sand which have been excavated from their burrows. Alert travelers can see these rodents sitting upright on their mounds watching for danger. If a hawk, coyote, or even a tourist approaches, they give a quick, shrill warning whistle and disappear. Prairie Dogs feed mainly on grass and other green vegetation. The two groups (White-tailed and Black-tailed) both have heavy-

White-tailed Prairie Dog

set bodies, rounded heads, and coarse fur. *Length:* 14 to 17 in. Females slightly smaller than males, but otherwise similar. They have four to six young in spring. The Black-tailed Prairie Dog, the more common species, is seen in the lower prairies. It is rusty yellow with a black-tipped tail. The White-tailed Prairie Dog is slightly smaller, with a white-tipped tail. It prefers higher mesas and mountains and does not make conspicuous mounds.

White-tailed
(former range)

Black-tailed
(former range)

Black-tailed Prairie Dog

EASTERN CHIPMUNKS are abundant in woodlands. They scamper from log to log, nervous and alert. They eat nuts, seeds, fruit, and—now and then—an insect. Eastern Chipmunks are ground-loving, though they may climb into shrubs and lower branches of trees. They dig long, shallow burrows, which include a nesting chamber. Three to five young are born about 30 days after mating and leave the nest a month later. *Adult length:* 9 to

10 in.; females similar to males. Voice is a low-pitched "chuck" often heard before the chipmunk is seen. They are active during the day, inactive on cold days.

a. **Colorado subspecies**

b. **Nevada subspecies**

LEAST CHIPMUNK is a small (*length:* 6 to 9 in.), variable western species, the most widely distributed of the chipmunks. All the dozen or more subspecies have stripes extending to the base of the tail. Color varies from dull yellow to gray brown. The eastern forms have richer-colored stripes. Least Chipmunks run with tail upright. They prefer more open country than Eastern Chipmunks.

c. **Midwestern subspecies**

CHIPMUNKS all have striped backs and cheeks. Most are curious and friendly, and can be enticed to take a nut or grain of corn from the hand. Their economic value is limited, but forests would not be the same without them. Of about 65 forms, those below and on pp. 78-79 are common and representative.

Townsend Chipmunk (9 to 11 in.), large, generally dark, has black stripes in its gray fur. Commonest in northwestern forests and high Sierras.

Cliff Chipmunk lives at lower altitudes, preferring piñon pine mesas. Stripes are indistinct except for a black one down the middle of the back. Color grayish.

Yellow-pine Chipmunk, of higher altitudes in western forests, is brown, with distinct black-and-white stripes, including a black stripe through the eye. Feeds on pine seeds and seeds of Mountain Mahogany.

Colorado Chipmunk is a western species, preferring higher mountains. (*Length:* 8 to 10 in.; *weight:* 2 to 2½ oz.) Typical chipmunk color with grayish-brown sides, tail darker and tipped with black. Most common in the Yellow Pine forests. Closely related to Umbrous Chipmunk.

1. Townsend Chipmunk

2. Cliff Chipmunk

4. Colorado Chipmunk

3. Yellow-pine Chipmunk

Outdoor nest

Indoor nest

RED SQUIRRELS (or Spruce or Pine Squirrels) are our smallest tree squirrels. They inhabit coniferous forests, filling them with noisy chatter. Summer color is duller, with a black line along the sides. Winter fur is brighter, and distinct ear tufts develop; no other eastern squirrel has them. Red Squirrels eat seeds, nuts, fruit, cones, insects, mushrooms, occasionally eggs. They build a nest of leaves in a tree hole or an empty woodpecker nest. Three to six young, born in spring, are mature by fall. *Length:* 11 to 14 in.

Winter pelage

CHICKAREES or DOUGLAS SQUIRRELS are agile tree-dwellers, found in the tall pines and spruces of the Northwest. In feeding they gnaw the stems of green cones till the cones drop to the ground. Then they climb down to harvest. The seeds are dug from the cones or, if the squirrel has fed, the cones are hidden away. The Chickaree, resembling the eastern Red Squirrel, has the same loud, chattering call. The underparts are reddish brown; the upper parts are rusty in winter, olive brown in summer, at which time there is also a black line on the sides. Litters of about five are born in June. Young can care for themselves by fall.

1. Eastern Gray Squirrel

GRAY SQUIRRELS, so often seen in parks, are found throughout the East and in the far West. The Western Gray Squirrel is larger but otherwise similar. No other tree squirrels are large and gray. Gray and other tree squirrels do not hibernate as ground squirrels do. An all-black form of the Eastern Gray Squirrel may be seen in parks. A bulky nest is built in forks of trees or in a hollow trunk. Four to six young are born in each litter.

Western

Arizona   Eastern

2. Western Gray Squirrel

**Black phase of
Eastern Gray Squirrel**

1. **North of Grand Canyon**

TUFT-EARED or ABERT SQUIRRELS, larger than Gray Squirrels (*length:* 19 to 21 in.), are confined to Yellow Pine forests of the Southwest. These pines provide food and nest sites. All have tufts on ears, with tufts more prominent in winter. These are our most attractive squirrels. On the north side of Grand Canyon lives an isolated group, the Kaibab Squirrels, with the tail nearly completely white; elsewhere tails are blackish or gray above, white below.

2. **South of Grand Canyon**

85

FOX SQUIRRELS are the largest of the tree squirrel group (*length:* 19 to 25 in.). They live on forest borders, feeding on acorns, fruit, seeds, and corn. Fox Squirrels vary in color. They are commonly a buff color with gray on the sides. Some are almost entirely gray. Occasionally, these squirrels are nearly black except for white spots on the head. The nests, large and bulky, are built in tree forks or in tree cavities. Usually two litters of two to five young are born each year.

Southern phase

Eastern phase

Northern phase

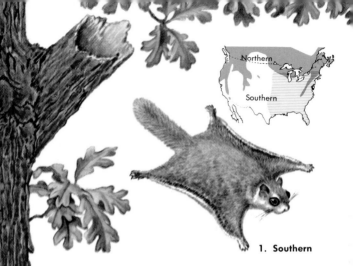

1. Southern

FLYING SQUIRRELS are small, drab-brown above, white below, with a loose fold of skin extending from the front to rear legs. They do not fly, but glide by extending their limbs and stretching the membrane between. Flying Squirrels, in contrast to others, are almost entirely nocturnal. Their diet includes animal matter, nuts, and fruit. Fur is soft and silky; eyes are large.

2. Northern

Incisors without grooves, short claws, (1). Western Pocket Gopher

Incisors with two grooves, long claws, (2). Plains Pocket Gopher

Incisors with one groove, long claws, (3). Yellow-faced Pocket Gopher

POCKET GOPHERS are burrowing rodents with short, naked tails and fur-lined cheek pouches for carrying food. With their powerful, clawed front legs they dig tunnels, which they seldom or never leave. If the burrow is extended to the surface, small mounds of dirt are thrown up. Food is roots and stems. Gophers (about 260 varieties) are of three major groups (genera): Western, Plains, and Yellow-faced. *Length: 7 to 13 in.*

88

1. Pallid Kangaroo Mouse

KANGAROO MICE are found mainly in Nevada. They are good jumpers and look like miniature Kangaroo Rats (pp. 92–93). Their unusual tail is thicker in the middle than at either end. Hind feet are long and hairy. Both Pallid and Dark species are animals of hot arid regions, where they feed on seeds of desert plants. Nocturnal in habit, they dig burrows under sage, rabbitbrush, or other shrubs. Their shallow burrows are closed from within during the daytime. Identification is difficult, since Kangaroo Mice may be easily confused with Pocket Mice, which are in the same family.

2. Dark Kangaroo Mouse

1. Hispid Pocket Mouse

POCKET MICE are all small rodents (*length:* 3½ to 6 in.). The 20 or more species have small ears, and tails that often end in hairy tufts. Pocket Mice vary in color from whitish to black, though most are grayish brown. Like their relatives, the Kangaroo Mice and Rats, Pocket Mice have external, fur-lined cheek pouches opening on either side of their small mouths. These western animals prefer arid regions. Burrows are dug for shelter and raising young. The burrow opening is often plugged up with earth during the day. Silky Pocket Mice are among

2. Apache Pocket Mouse

1. Long-tailed Pocket Mouse

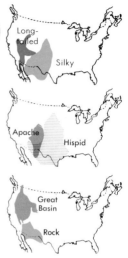

2. Great Basin Pocket Mouse

our smallest mammals. Some Pocket Mice live in sand, others among rocks or brush. All are poor jumpers. Pocket Mice get enough water from the dry seeds and plant matter they eat and so are able to get along for months without drinking. Many are dormant during cold weather.

3. Rock Pocket Mouse

KANGAROO RATS are unique rodents with long, over-developed hind limbs and shorter, less developed forelimbs. They move rapidly with long, kangaroo-like leaps, keeping their front legs off the ground. Their large heads, long tufted tails, white flank stripes, white on the sides of the tail, and white belly are distinctive markings that make Kangaroo Rats easy to recognize. Most species are found in

1. Ord Kangaroo Rat

2. Banner-tailed Kangaroo Rat

Merriam and relatives

Banner-tailed

1. **Merriam Kangaroo Rat**

the Southwest; all inhabit dry regions, living in burrows dug into the soil. They are nocturnal, feed mainly on seeds and dry vegetation, and are preyed upon by carnivores, owls, and snakes. Like the Pocket Mice, Kangaroo Rats can get along with very little water. Litters of two to four young are born during spring and summer. Of 16 or more species, typical are: Merriam, Desert, and Banner-tailed Kangaroo Rats, with four toes on each hind foot; Ord, with five.

2. **Desert Kangaroo Rat**

Ord

Desert

93

Front

Hind

BEAVERS dam streams with sticks and mud to form ponds around their big, one-room houses with underwater entrances. At night they gnaw down trees and float branches through canals to the ponds. Beavers eat the fresh inner bark and also water plants, and store branches underwater for winter food. They mate for life. The young (two to six) are born in spring. Beaver pelts are valuable; their dams are important in flood control.

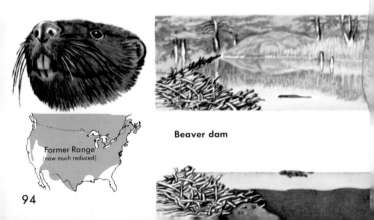

Former Range
(now much reduced)

Beaver dam

Juvenile

Adult

GRASSHOPPER MICE, as their name indicates, feed mainly on grasshoppers and other insects—an unusual diet for rodents. They are fat-bodied, with thick, tapering, white-tipped tails, which are short in the northern species and over half the body length in the southern species. These mice are inhabitants of plains and desert grasslands, and nest in burrows below ground.

Northern

Southern

Beaver house

1. Western Harvest Mouse

HARVEST MICE, brownish with grayish-brown undersides and gray legs, are small (*length:* 4 to 6 in.), House-Mouse size, but with grooved upper incisors. They inhabit the South and warmer parts of the West. They build a ball-like nest of grass in meadows, on the ground, or slightly above it, and raise several litters a year. Western Harvest Mouse occurs in arid regions. Eastern Harvest Mouse is found in damp meadows and thickets. Harvest Mice are all seed eaters and are less common than Deer Mice.

2. Eastern Harvest Mouse

1. Golden Mouse

GOLDEN MICE of the Southeast are a rich golden brown—hence the name—with white underparts. These small mice (body about 3¾ in. and tail about 3 in.) are tree- and shrub-dwelling species, usually in pine-cedar-greenbrier-honeysuckle. They build their round, compact nests of grasses and leaves high in these shrubs and trees. Several mice may inhabit one nest.

CACTUS MICE dwell in the hot deserts of the Southwest, living among rocks, cacti, and desert scrub. When water is unavailable, these mice go into a water-conserving torpor.

2. Cactus Mouse

Cactus   Golden

97

1. White-footed Mouse

WHITE-FOOTED and DEER MICE represent a wide-spread group of small to medium-sized, white-footed, white-bellied mice. Most are brownish or brownish gray. The White-footed Mouse is a more eastern species of open woodlands and scrubby hillsides. Deer Mice have a wider range, living in open areas and in woods. These mice eat seeds, plants, insects. Nests are beneath rocks and logs, in burrows, or in trees.

Deer

White-footed

2. Deer Mouse

Juvenile

Adult

98

RICE RATS are larger editions of White-footed Mice, but look like young rats. They have whitish feet, grayish bellies, and long tails, which are lighter in color underneath. They live and nest in salt- and fresh-water marshes, feeding on a variety of plants. Their liking of rice plants has earned them their name. They are excellent swimmers. Rice rats are common but nocturnal. Young are born in a grass nest. The Marsh Rice Rat is most widespread in the U.S.; more species are in Central America.

Marsh

99

1. Desert Woodrat

WOODRATS look a bit like Norway Rats (p. 112), but these native species have a more hairy tail; the feet and throat are whiter. There are also important differences in the teeth. The widespread Eastern Woodrats live in caves and cliffs. In the West, woodrats occur from the deserts to the mountains. All are nocturnal. They build large nests, collecting all sorts of objects to incorporate in them. This habit gives the name Pack Rats to western species. The result is often a large mound of sticks and

Bushy-tailed

Desert and relatives

2. White-throated Woodrat

1. Bushy-tailed Woodrat

rubbish laid between rocks. Travelers hear many stories of things these rats have stolen and hidden away. White-throated Woodrats often build nests under cacti. The Bushy-tailed Woodrat may nest in the attic of a mountain cabin. Occasionally, nests are made in trees. Woodrats raise two or three litters of two or three young each season. Woodrats feed on fruits, berries, and seeds, and eat the leaves and stalks of many plants.

White-throated / Eastern and relatives

2. Eastern Woodrat

Hispid Cotton Rat

COTTON RATS are shaggy-furred, small rats of grassy or weedy places. They are abundant in the South, where they damage truck gardens and farm crops. They are active during the day as well as at night. The Hispid Cotton Rat is most common, preferring the shelter of tall meadow grass, hedgerows, and roadside ditches. Well-marked trails lead from burrows to feeding areas. Yellow-nosed Cotton Rats live in mountain meadows. Fulvous Cotton Rats are tan-colored below. These rats may have six litters a year, each of six or more young, which begin to leave the nest after about a week. If weeds and other cover are cleared away, hawks, owls, and carnivores can better control the rats.

Hispid

BOG LEMMINGS are not the true lemmings but are similar to voles (pp. 104-106). Their grooved incisors are the best distinguishing characteristic. Bog Lemmings are northern rodents preferring moist sphagnum bogs, swamps, and forest meadows. They are small (*length:* 4 to 5½ in., including a tail 1 in. long, or less). Their fur is thick and fine, nearly covering the small ears. Food is mainly grass, though bulbs and perhaps insects are eaten. Bog Lemmings live in colonies. Runways connect the nests, which are built in tussocks of grass. They also dig burrows through the moist earth or through the packed sphagnum. Several litters (four to six young in each) are raised each season.

Southern Bog Lemming

1. **Red-backed Vole**

2. **Meadow Vole**

3. **Mountain Vole**

4. **California Vole**

Meadow

California

Red-backed and relatives

Mountain

(Text on page 106.)

1. Sagebrush Vole

2. Long-tailed Vole

3. Prairie Vole

4. Pine Vole

Long-tailed

Sagebrush

Prairie

Pine
and relatives

(Text on page 106.)

Rock Vole

VOLES, often called Field or Meadow Mice, are the most common and most prolific of the rodents. One female in captivity had 17 litters a year. Litters range from three to ten young. Young voles can care for themselves when 12 days old and can breed in less than a month. Most voles are gray, some tinged with brown. They average 5 to 7 in. long, with short tails, small ears, and black beady eyes. The Meadow Vole is widespread in eastern and northern states. The Red-backed Vole, of forests in both eastern and western mountains, spreads far into the north. The California Vole, in the fertile river valleys, is one of the species that sometimes becomes a serious pest. When food conditions are favorable, the population in these meadows has increased to many hundreds per acre. Pine Voles live in the leaf mold of our eastern forests; Sagebrush Voles, in colonies among the desert sage.

Voles build nests of grass on the ground. Here they raise litter after litter throughout a breeding season which lasts as long as the climate permits. A maze of narrow runways made by clipping the grass along the way extends through the fields. Voles eat grass, grain, and almost every other kind of plant material. In winter they girdle young trees and damage orchard and nursery stock.

Collared Lemming (winter)

LEMMINGS are found throughout arctic and sub-arctic regions. They are the most common northern rodents. Brown and Collared Lemmings live in the stunted forests and tundras. Both occur in Alaska and adjacent parts of northern Canada. The Collared Lemming is the only rodent that turns white in winter. Lemmings are important food for Arctic Foxes. Like some rabbits and other rodents, the lemming population rises and falls in cycles. These lemmings do not undergo migrations as do Norwegian lemmings. With the latter, a population rise culminates in a migration to seek new territory. Predators follow the movement, taking great toll.

1. Collared Lemming (summer)   2. Brown Lemming

1. Red Tree Vole

HEATHER VOLES are northern rodents of Canada, Alaska, and some of our northwestern mountains. They live along streams, in mountain meadows, and one species (the Red Tree Vole) lives mostly in trees, building a nest high on the branches of some conifers. All have grayish-brown, soft fur and short tails except for the Red Tree Vole, which is reddish with a long, dark, hairy tail. Heather Voles are considered rare, though careful observation indicates they are more common than once believed. The group is often called by the genus name *Phenacomys*, because there is no well-established common name.

2. Heather Vole

FLORIDA WATER RAT is often called Round-tailed Muskrat. Found only in Florida and nearby parts of Georgia, this interesting rodent can be identified by its size (*length:* 13 to 15 in.) and by its long (5 in.), round tail. It has fine, dark brown fur, but the small size precludes its being trapped for its pelt. Water rats are found in bogs and along lake-shores, and never far from water. They are excellent swimmers. A round nest about a foot in diameter is built in mangrove roots or between cypress knees. Runways spread from the nest through the swamp grass and bog sphagnum. Water rats feed on all kinds of swamp vegetation. Because of the warm climate they may breed all year round.

MUSKRATS are well-known rodents, producing more fur pelts than all other American mammals combined. They are closely related to the voles (*average length:* 23 in., with their slightly flattened 10-in. tail). Muskrats build large houses in shallow water or burrow into stream banks. In these shelters several litters (two to nine young in each) are raised each season. The principal food is cattail roots and stalks. They also eat several other swamp plants, some clams, and fish.

Muskrat house

APLODONTIA is often called Mountain Beaver—a misleading name, for it is no beaver. It does live in the redwood and spruce forests of the northwest mountains. A fair swimmer, it prefers damp localities, often near streams, where it digs shallow burrows. A variety of mountain plants are used as food, and the surplus is often piled near the mouth of the burrow. Three or four young are born in spring. *Length:* 12 to 15 in. Tail very short. The fur is short but attractive.

111

Norway Rat

RATS and MICE that most people know are introduced Old World rodents. These successful mammals have adapted themselves to us and have lived and traveled with men for centuries. Thousands upon thousands of

deaths can be directly attributed to disease spread by rats, and millions upon millions of dollars damage has been done by them. The Norway Rat is 12 to 20 in. long, with a bare, scaly tail slightly

1. House Mouse

shorter than its body. It lacks the white belly of our
native woodrat. The Black Rat is slightly smaller, more
slender, and has a tail longer than the body. A lighter-
colored but less common form of the Black Rat, with
brownish fur, is the Roof or Alexandrian Rat. The House
Mouse, much smaller than rats (5 to 7 in. long, with a 3-
to 4-in. tail), is even more common in homes, though it
often lives in fields along with native species of mice. Its
gray color, including underparts, and long naked tail
make identification easy, even if the animal is scurry-
ing across the kitchen floor. Albino (white) mice and
Norway rats are used constantly in scientific research.

2. Black Rat

113

1. **Western Jumping Mouse**

JUMPING MICE are small, long-tailed, jumping species that prefer moist, grassy meadows where, if disturbed, they can leap to safety, using their long hind legs and balancing tails. Although resembling Kangaroo Rats (pp. 92-93), they are smaller (head and body, 3 to 4 in.; tail, 5 to 6 in.), lack a bushy tail, and are not desert dwellers. Jumping Mice hibernate in winter; most other mice do not. Food is almost entirely grass seeds and small plants. There are three types: Western, Meadow, and Woodland Jumping Mice. The last occurs in deep forests and has a conspicuous white tip on the tail. Five or six young are born in one litter, late in spring.

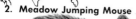

2. **Meadow Jumping Mouse**

3. **Woodland Jumping Mouse**

114

PORCUPINES are large (*length:* up to 30 in.; *weight:* to 40 lb.), clumsy rodents, recognized at once. The spines, especially on the back and tail, are loosely attached. They are barbed and can seriously injure or kill an attacking animal. Spines are not quills, but modified hairs, and are not shot out by the porcupine. Porcupines feed on wood and inner bark of many trees, and eat additional plant food in summer.

NUTRIA are large, brownish South American rodents, 30 to 42 in. long. They were brought into this country about 1900 as a promising fur animal and were released in muskrat swamps. Nutria, aquatic animals, swim well and thrive in swamps. Their fur is widely used. Nutria are now well established in parts of Louisiana and are present in some other states. They are steadily spreading

into new areas. Can be distinguished from muskrats (p. 110) by larger size and round tails. Nutria eat more varied food than muskrats and in some places are reported as replacing muskrats.

RABBITS

HARES

ROCK HARES

PIKAS

THE RABBIT FAMILY consists of pikas, hares, and rabbits. All have four sharp, curved incisors in the upper jaw, while rodents have only two. Rabbits are widespread, adaptable, and are able to survive in everything from hedgerows to suburban yards. When introduced into Australia, they all but took over the continent. Hares and rabbits are confusing. In general, the hares are long-legged, high-jumping, with young born well furred and with eyes open. Rabbits, born naked and blind, are short-legged, running species.

Newborn rabbit

Newborn hare

117

Winter pelage

Fall

Spring

VARYING HARE or SNOWSHOE RABBIT is an example of name confusion. The animal is a hare—two to six young are born with eyes open and fully furred. However, its ears are relatively short. The word "Varying" refers to color changes that occur from summer to winter. "Snowshoe" refers to the wide, furry paws, which give the hare a good footing on ice and in soft snow. These hares (*length:* 13 to 18 in.) feed on grass and soft plants in summer. In winter they may chew bark off young trees, killing many. The hare population rises and falls in little-understood cycles.

Summer

118

EUROPEAN HARES, also called Cape Hares, were imported into Ontario and spread south into some of our northern states. They have been introduced also into the Hudson valley. This large hare, 25 to 30 in. long, has disproportionately large feet and head. European Hares prefer open country and have become abundant near farms and orchards, where they may cause serious winter damage to fruit trees. The phrase "mad as a March Hare" refers to the males, which in early spring leap, tumble, and fight as a preliminary to mating.

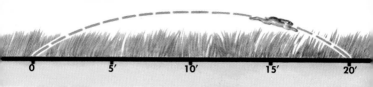

| 0 | 5' | 10' | 15' | 20' |

Leap of White-tailed Jackrabbit

JACKRABBITS are native western hares. Famed in story, these long-eared, long-legged creatures look like caricatures, but they are well adapted to life in semi-arid country. Jackrabbits feed on almost every kind of vegetation, and can get along with very little water. Occasionally they do damage to alfalfa and grain fields. Ears, sometimes a third of the hare's length, keep it aware of its many enemies. Jackrabbits are a main item in the diet of Coyotes. When frightened, these hares may leap high in the air, perhaps to get a view

White-tailed Jackrabbit

of things. When pursued they run with powerful leaps of 15 to 20 ft. at a measured speed of over 40 miles per hour. The White-tailed Jackrabbit is the largest native species (*length:* 18 to 22 in.; *weight:* 5 to 8 lb.). Fur turns paler or changes completely to white in winter. Tail is white the year round. The Black-tailed Jackrabbit is slightly smaller, prefers more open ground, and is marked by a black streak on the tail and by black-tipped ears. It prefers a warmer climate than the White-tail. The Antelope Jackrabbit of the southwest desert is related to the Blacktail, but with even larger ears, which have no black at the tip. The white on its rump and side flashes as it leaps. All Jackrabbits browse on bark, twigs, buds, and any soft plant food that is available.

1. Antelope Jackrabbit

2. Black-tailed Jackrabbit

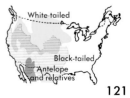

White-tailed

Black-tailed

Antelope
and relatives

COTTONTAILS are the true rabbits, found nearly every-where in this country. In size they are generally small (*length:* 11 to 17 in.; *weight:* 2 to 4 lb.). Eyes are dark, ears and legs short. Nearly all have the white "cottontail" that gives the group its name. These rabbits take over vacant burrows or make shelters in brush heaps. Litters average four or five naked, blind babies, which are big enough to leave the nest in about two weeks, leave their mother in less than two months, and are mature in six months. Several litters a year are common. Nests of young cottontails are better left alone. Some species, such as the Eastern Cottontail, do well in

Hind

Front

122

1. Desert Cottontail

2. Brush Rabbit

close proximity with humans, living in cities, feeding on gardens and lawns.

The Eastern Cottontail is a well-known species. Its range in the South overlaps that of the slightly larger Marsh and Swamp Rabbits (p. 124). The Brush Rabbit of the Pacific Coast (*length:* 11 to 13 in.) and the Desert Cottontail of the inland West (*length:* 12 to 15 in.) are somewhat smaller species. The Brush Rabbit is a brownish species found on brush-covered hillsides. The Desert Cottontail, grayer and paler, is most common in river valleys of the Southwest.

3. Eastern Cottontail

Brush Rabbit

Desert Cottontail

Eastern Cottontail

1. **Swamp Rabbit**

MARSH RABBIT is a southern species about the same size as the Eastern Cottontail. To identify it in the field, note the tail is small and grayish beneath. Its color is dark brown, including the small feet, which contrast with the lighter-colored feet of the Eastern Cottontail. These rabbits live in marshes and feed on marsh grasses. The Swamp Rabbit lives in similar habitats in the lower Mississippi Valley and along the Gulf. In color it is intermediate between the Eastern Cottontail and the Marsh Rabbit—a brownish gray with reddish-brown feet.

2. **Marsh Rabbit**

PYGMY RABBIT is our smallest cottontail, found in a limited area of the dry western uplands. Its small size (about 11 in.) is a clue for field identification. It is a weak jumper. In color, it resembles the Eastern Cottontail—gray, tinged with brown. It lives in tall, dense sagebrush and rabbitbrush and digs small burrows in the ground. Brush and burrows afford these rabbits protection from owls, hawks, and coyotes. They rarely stray far from sagebrush, on which they feed. They often live in colonies, breed in spring (perhaps again in late summer), with litters of about six.

PIKAS or CONIES are not rabbits but belong in a separate family. They are rabbit-like; small (*length:* 7 to 8 in.) and seemingly tail-less. Pikas live high in the western mountains. A related species lives in Alaska. Pikas are more active than rabbits during the day. They feed on grass and gather the surplus into conspicuous hay mounds. Their whistling call is something like the Marmot's. The color of Pikas blends so with the rocks in which they usually live that they are hard to see even though they sit hunched up in the sun. Three or four young arrive in late spring or early summer.

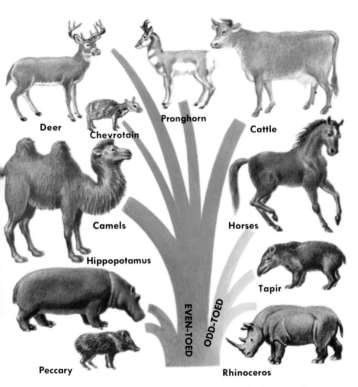

Deer

Chevrotain

Pronghorn

Cattle

Camels

Horses

Hippopotamus

Tapir

EVEN-TOED

ODD-TOED

Peccary

Rhinoceros

HOOFED MAMMALS (ungulates), mainly large plant-eaters, are important. We ride them, use them as beasts of burden, eat their flesh, make leather from their hides, drink their milk. As our frontiers pushed west, many species almost vanished. Now hunting is controlled and some are again plentiful. Single-toed ungulates include horses and kin, tapirs, and rhinoceros. The two-toed or split-hoofed group includes all wild species now living in America: the pronghorn, cattle and bison, deer, and pig families.

127

1. Bison

2. Bighorn

3. Pronghorn

HORNS AND ANTLERS, grown by some hoofed mammals, serve for defense or for mating battles.

Antlers are solid bony growths from the skull, found on male deer, elk, and moose, and on both sexes of caribou. They grow in spring under a layer of living skin—the velvet. Later this peels off. The antlers themselves are shed each year. The following spring a new, larger set grows.

Horns have a bony core over which the horn (similar to your fingernails) grows. Horns are not shed, and increase in size with each new year's growth. Cattle, bison, mountain sheep, and goats have horns. The Pronghorn's unusual horns are shed each year and a new horny covering grows over the bone. They are the only horns that are pronged or branched.

4. Moose

5. Caribou

COLLARED PECCARIES are relatives of the pigs and, together with the more southern White-lipped Peccary, are the only animals of their kind in the New World. Small (*length:* 38 in.), tough, sometimes vicious, they live in herds of 12 or more. Peccaries are not cud-chewers, but root out plants, feeding on fruits, nuts, insects, lizards, and snakes. The slightly curved tusks are used in defense. Peccaries emit a strong odor from musk glands near the tail. Male and female are much alike. One or two young are born at a time. Wild boars (unrelated) have been introduced in several places.

MULE DEER, a western species, up to 6 ft. long and 4 ft. high at the shoulders, weighs up to 350 lb. The doe (female) is smaller. Twins, or sometimes one or three fawns, born in late spring, stay with her through the next winter, sometimes longer. Mule Deer browse, *i.e.* feed on twigs and leaves. They sometimes graze on grass and eat wild fruits. Bucks (males) summer in higher mountains, coming down to mate in late fall. The herd remains together much of the winter. By early spring, does leave to bear young. Mule Deer, often seen in

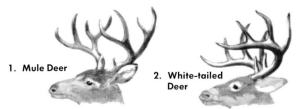

1. Mule Deer
2. White-tailed Deer

western National Parks, are of several varieties, Black-tailed (with distinct black tail) being best known. This somewhat smaller deer occurs in the Northwest and up into Alaska.

3. Mule Deer

4. Black-tailed Deer

Black-tailed (related)

Mule

131

White-tailed buck

WHITE-TAILED or VIRGINIA DEER is the most common deer and one of the best-known and most admired game animals. The first game laws enacted in colonial days were to protect it. White-tailed Deer are reddish-brown, becoming more gray in winter. The fawns, born in late spring (earlier in the South), remain spotted with white for 4 to 5 months. Bucks are about 5 ft. long and 3 ft. high at shoulder, weigh up to 250 lb., rarely more.

Does are smaller. Antlers, on males only, spread forward distinctively (see p. 131). Both male and female have long (12-in.) tails, white under-

1. White-tailed doe and fawns

neath. These are raised like white flags when deer are in flight. White-tailed Deer are browsers, feeding on leaves and twigs, water plants, acorns, and other fruits. In winter they gather together in "deer yards." Under protection, Whitetails have increased and are now plentiful. Among the subspecies are two dwarf kinds: the Coues Deer of Arizona and the Key Deer of Big Pine Key in southern Florida. The Key Deer, not much bigger than a large collie, were hunted till they were close to extinction. Now the population is recovering, but still in danger.

2. Key Deer

BISON, often known as Buffalo, are the largest wild animals in America. A big bull, 6 ft. high at the shoulder and 10 ft. long, weighs over a ton. The female (cow) is smaller. Both bull and cow have horns. Great herds totaling over 60 million animals once roamed the plains, spreading into eastern and northern forests. Travelers reported herds as vast as the eye could see. But Bison were killed for sport, food, hides, bones—and to help control the Plains Indians, who depended on Bison for food. By 1820 the animals had been exterminated east of the Mississippi; by 1885 all that remained of the

great Western herds was about 75 animals. These survivors, protected on reservations, have now increased to several thousand. The hump-shouldered bulls, always wary, protect the herd and mate with cows during the summer. Calves (one and occasionally twins) are born the following spring and stay with their mother through the next winter. The Woodland Bison is a larger and darker-colored subspecies, now found only in western Canada.

Originally
In 1850
In 1870
In 1880

ELK or WAPITI (an Algonkin Indian name) are large American deer with widespreading antlers and a thick mane. Males stand 5 ft. high at shoulder and weigh over 600 lb. Females are smaller, lacking antlers. Bulls fight off rivals and collect a herd of cows. One or two spotted young are born to each cow, late in the spring. Herds migrate more than other deer, moving into the mountains during summer.

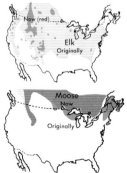

Now (red)

Elk
Originally

Moose
Now

Originally

MOOSE are the largest American deer (*length*: 9 ft.; *height*: 6 ft.; *weight*: about 1,000 lb.). Female, much smaller, lacks broad, flattened antlers of male. Moose are northern animals, favoring moist lowlands, often feeding on water plants in lakes and streams. In winter they stay closer to forests. One (rarely two) young is born in late spring and stays with its mother almost a year. She chases it away just before her new calf arrives. Moose are also found in Europe, where they are called Elk.

CARIBOU are large northern and arctic deer with heavy antlers (smaller on female) and shaggy fur on belly and neck. They are short-tailed. The young are not spotted, as in other deer. Males are about 6 ft. long, 4 ft. high, and weigh 300 lb. or more. The Woodland and Barren-ground Caribou are the two major types living in Canada and Alaska. Reindeer, a semi-domesticated European subspecies now established in Alaska, is another kind of Caribou. Eskimos tend the herds of Reindeer, which are steadily increasing.

Woodland
Now (yellow)

Barren-ground
Now (red)

Woodland Caribou

MOUNTAIN GOATS are more like antelopes than true goats and are related to the Chamois of the Alps. Short-horned, shaggy-coated animals, they prefer high mountain regions, where they feed on moss and alpine grasses. These sure-footed beasts seem able to climb impossible ledges. Males grow to about 5 ft. long, over 3 ft. high; females smaller. Both males and females have short, dark, curved horns. One or two young are born in late spring. Exceedingly rare.

139

BIGHORN SHEEP live in western mountains on the rocky slopes and crags, where they are safest from wolves and coyotes. They climb, sure-footed, on two-toed, cushioned hoofs. Their brownish-gray, deer-like coats make them almost invisible against the rocks. Bighorns feed on grass and shrubs. During the mating season, rams fight, and sometimes a general rough-and-tumble develops. The females have one or two young, born in spring, which quickly become self-reliant. Bighorns live in bands of six or more. *Length:* to 6 ft.; *height:* over 3 ft.; *weight:* to 225 lb.; female smaller. Both sexes have horns.

Originally

Now (red)

PRONGHORNS are truly American, for these swift, graceful animals have no close relatives elsewhere. Though often called antelopes, Pronghorns do not belong to that Old World group, but are more closely related to sheep. Pronghorns are the only horned mammals that shed the outer covering of their horns each year. The unusual white rump patch makes them easy to spot from a distance. In frontier days Pronghorns were easily killed, for their curiosity led them close to hunters. Sizable herds still remain on the western plains. Two fawns are born in late spring. *Weight:* 110 lb; *length:* 5 ft., *shoulder height:* 3 ft.

Originally

Now (red)

Federal refuges (dots)

ARMADILLOS, our oddest mammals, are covered, except for their ears and legs, by bony plates. Unlike some South American species, our Nine-banded Armadillo cannot curl up into a ball for protection. To avoid coyotes and peccaries, it digs a hole or seeks refuge in thorny tangles. Armadillos are most active at night. Their long, sticky tongues catch insects. When insects are lacking, they may starve. In spring, litters of four identical young (always of the same sex) are born. Their skin is like soft leather at first. The bony plates do not harden until the young are fully grown. Armadillo flesh makes good eating; it tastes like pork. *Length: to 30 in.; weight:* 15 lb.

Now
(red)

By 1875
(blue)

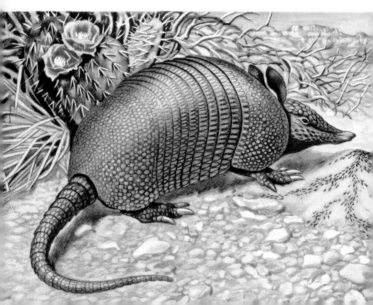

MANATEES (SEA COWS)

are the sirens of fables and sailors' yarns. Really they are large, slow, bald-headed, and timid—hardly alluring. Manatees live solely on aquatic plants in shallow coastal waters. Their forelegs are modified into flippers. Hind legs are absent, and the body ends in a broad, flattened, not ungraceful tail. The single young, born in a sheltered lagoon, is able to swim right after birth. It often nurses under water, coming up for air every minute or so. *Length:* 10 to 12 ft.; *weight:* up to about a ton.

143

1. Baleen

2. Toothed

WHALES AND THEIR KIN form a large group, found in all the open seas and along many shores. A few even live in rivers and fresh-water lakes. They range from small, 5-ft. dolphins to the great Blue Whales, which have occasionally reached 100 ft. in length and 115 tons in weight. These, the largest animals that have ever lived, dwarf the great dinosaurs and weigh as much as 20 to 30 elephants.

Whales and their kin are descendants of land animals. Their skeleton shows the remains of a pelvic girdle, but all outward traces of hind legs have been lost. The front limbs are modified into flippers concealing the bones, which show that once five fingers were present. The tail developed into horizontal flukes (in contrast to the vertical tail fins of fish).

Whales have been harpooned and hunted for their flesh and other by-products (oil, whalebone, ambergris) for centuries. Methods of hunting them today, especially with helicopters and fleets of ships, make them easy targets and highly vulnerable. Because of their slow reproductive rate, this harvesting can be threatening to the species, especially if the take is high. For the last several years, many kinds of whales have been on the verge of extinction, and international efforts have been made to control whaling. Limits have been set on the number of individuals of each species that can be taken annually. By 1988, it is hoped that all commercial taking of whales will be stopped, although some aboriginal groups, such as Siberian and American eskimos, will be permitted to take a limited number.

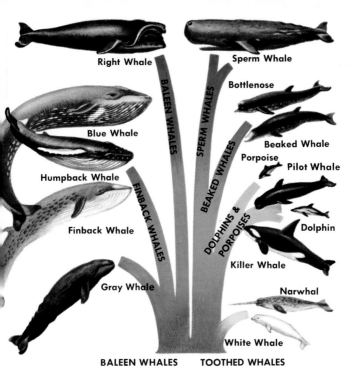

Right Whale

Sperm Whale

Blue Whale

Bottlenose

Humpback Whale

Beaked Whale

Porpoise

Pilot Whale

Finback Whale

Dolphin

Gray Whale

Killer Whale

Narwhal

White Whale

BALEEN WHALES   TOOTHED WHALES

(Labels within figure: BALEEN WHALES, SPERM WHALES, BEAKED WHALES, FINBACK WHALES, DOLPHINS & PORPOISES)

Like all mammals, whales breathe air and must come to the surface to "blow" or breathe. After a long blow, large whales can stay under for about an hour. Whales are so adapted to ocean life that the skeleton cannot support the body on land. Whales soon die when stranded on a beach. At birth there is but one young; the mother nurses it as do other mammals.

The whales are divided into two distinct groups: the Baleen (Whalebone) or Toothless Whales, a small group of our largest whales (pp. 146-147), and the Toothed Whales (pp. 148-153), including dolphins and porpoises.

BALEEN WHALES (nine species) are giants, with paired blow-holes. Instead of teeth, they have rows of whalebone (baleen) hanging from the upper jaw. The whalebone traps millions of tiny sea animals for food.

Blue Whale (Sulphur-bottomed), largest whale known, prefers colder Atlantic and Pacific waters. Throat deeply furrowed. *Length:* 80 to 100 ft.; *weight:* to 115 tons.

Humpback Whale is short, heavy, with rough, irregular flippers and skin. Playful Humpbacks live in schools, leap and tumble in courtship. *Length:* 40 to 50 ft.

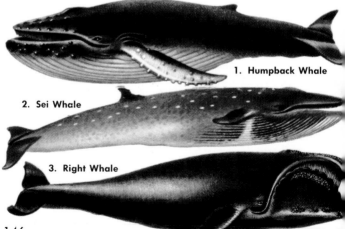

1. **Humpback Whale**

2. **Sei Whale**

3. **Right Whale**

1. Blue Whale

Sei Whales, which seem to migrate more than others, have a pleated throat like the Blue Whale's. *Length: 50 to 60 ft.*

Right Whale (the right one for whalers) is found mainly in northern oceans. It lacks the back (dorsal) fin of other large whales. *Length: 50 to 60 ft.*

Finback Whale is flat-headed, large, with a small dorsal fin. It spouts with a loud whistle. *Length: 60 to 70 ft.*

Gray Whale of the Pacific is frequently seen close to shore. Its gray skin is often mottled with white patches of barnacles. *Length: 30 to 40 ft.*

2. Finback Whale

3. Gray Whale

147

TOOTHED WHALES

SPERM WHALE is the largest of Toothed Whales, all of which have a single blow-hole. The square snout and head make up almost a third of the length. About 30 teeth, in the thin lower jaw, fit into sockets in the toothless upper jaw. The entire head is off balance. The bulky forehead contains a large "tank" of thin wax which, before the time of petroleum, was the main source of oil for lamps. The Sperm Whale was widely hunted in both

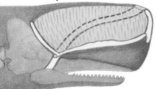

Sperm Whale oil case

Atlantic and Pacific, where it dives over half a mile deep in search of giant squid. It grows 40 to 60 ft. long, occasionally larger. Fabled Moby Dick was an albino Sperm Whale.

BEAKED WHALES are small to medium-sized Toothed Whales. Their teeth are actually few, sometimes only a single pair. They prefer colder waters of the open oceans and are seen only occasionally near shore.

True's Beaked Whale (15 to 20 ft.), named after a Mr. True, is less common along our shores than Bottlenose Whales. Males have one pair of teeth in lower jaw.

Bottlenose Whales (25 to 30 ft. long), most common of this group, were hunted for their fine oil after Sperm Whales became scarce. Found south to New England.

Goosebeak or Cuvier's Whale (15 to 20 ft.), variable in color and pattern, is found in all oceans.

1. **True's Beaked Whale**

2. **Bottlenose Whale: :
Old male (upper)
and mature male**

3. **Goosebeak Whale**

PORPOISES are smaller relatives of the dolphins. Active animals, they are often seen in schools. These small whales (*length:* 4 to 6 ft.) feed mainly on fish. The Harbor Porpoise is most common in the Atlantic, especially along shore, where it swims rapidly, often leaping clear of the water. It is black above, lighter beneath. Harbor Porpoises are also found in the Pacific.

The north Pacific boasts of the more attractive, somewhat larger (*length:* 5 to 6 ft.) Dall Porpoise. This species has a large white patch on the abdomen and sides of its otherwise black body. It prefers colder water than the Harbor Porpoise.

2. Harbor Porpoises

Pilot Whales

PILOT WHALES are a common porpoise of the Atlantic and Pacific. Three species, all 15 to 20 ft. long, live in schools in open ocean and along coasts. All are similar, though one has shorter flippers than the others. Their name comes from the fact that they travel in groups, closely following the leader. If by misfortune the leader heads for shoal water, the entire school follows, and all may become stranded on a beach. These whales are also called Ca'ing Whales or Blackfish. Pilot Whales have a single young, which is nearly half the size of the mother at birth. In the past, schools of them were hunted for their oil and for their flesh.

Pilot Whale

Killers attacking a baleen whale

DOLPHINS are small Toothed Whales with teeth in both jaws. About two dozen species live in waters off North America. The True Dolphins have snouts which project as beaks.

Killer Whales (*length:* 15 to 20 ft.) are large dolphins and the fiercest of marine animals. Traveling in schools, they attack other dolphins, porpoises, seals, and even Baleen Whales. Gray Whales are said to run aground to escape them. The False Killer Whale is smaller and lacks the black and white markings of the true Killer Whale.

Killer Whale

152

Common Dolphin (*length: 6 to 8 ft.*) is the one usually seen around the bow of ships. This attractive, dark gray animal, playful-looking but voracious, feeds on small fish. A closely related species lives in the Pacific.

Bottlenose Dolphin (*length: 9 to 12 ft.*), larger than others, has a shorter, stubbier beak. Commoner than Common Dolphin, it was once hunted for hides and oil. One Atlantic and one Pacific species are known.

Spotted Dolphin, about the size of Common Dolphin, has many white patches on its back. It occurs along the Atlantic Coast and the Gulf.

1. Common Dolphin

2. Bottlenose Dolphin

3. Spotted Dolphin

BOOKS FOR FURTHER STUDY Detailed accounts of the mammals of each of our 50 states are available for all except about a dozen. Various natural history magazines as well as the *Journal of Mammalogy* have more detailed information about mammals. Publications on particular mammals are available—bats, coyotes, white-tailed deer, fox squirrels, etc.

Burt, William H., A FIELD GUIDE TO THE MAMMALS, Houghton Mifflin Co., Boston, 3rd ed., 1976. An excellent field guide to 373 North American species, with illustrations, maps, life histories.

Hall, E. R., THE MAMMALS OF NORTH AMERICA. 2 vols. John Wiley & Sons, New York, 1981. Included are methods of identification, distribution maps, scientific and common names for all North American mammals.

Hamilton, W. J., AMERICAN MAMMALS, McGraw-Hill Book Co., New York, 1939, and Hamilton and J. O. Whitaker, Jr., THE MAMMALS OF EASTERN UNITED STATES, Comstock Pub. Co., Ithaca, N.Y., 1979. The first is a systematic introduction to mammalogy. The second is a popular yet thorough account of eastern land mammals.

ZOOS TO VISIT Zoos give an opportunity to study at first hand larger, more interesting mammals. Some are:

Chicago: Chicago Zoological Society, Brookfield Zoo.
Chicago: Lincoln Park Zoological Society.
New York: New York Zoological Society, Bronx Park.
Philadelphia: Philadelphia Zoological Park.
St. Louis: St. Louis Zoological Garden, Forest Park.
San Diego: San Diego Zoological Society, Balboa Park.
San Francisco: Fleischaker Zoo.
Washington: National Zoological Garden, Rock Creek.

MUSEUMS TO VISIT Here are some famous museums where the mammal exhibits are good. Museums are also found at many universities and state capitols.

Chicago: Field Museum.
Denver: Denv. Mus. of Nat. Hist.
Los Angeles: Nat. Hist. Mus.
Milwaukee: Milw. Public Museum.
New York: Amer. Mus. of Nat. Hist.

Pittsburgh: Carnegie Mus. Nat. Hist.
San Diego: S. D. Nat. Hist. Mus.
San Francisco: Calif. Acad. of Sci.
Washington, D.C.: Natl. Mus. Nat. Hist.

SCIENTIFIC NAMES

Specialists almost universally use the scientific names for species because these make possible more precision in designations. Following is a list of the scientific names of species illustrated in this book. Numbers in heavy type are numbers of pages on which species appear; numbers in lighter type refer to the numbered captions on those pages. The genus name appears first; the species name follows; if there is a third name, this is the subspecies. An alternate generic or species name is sometimes given in brackets: e.g., **34.** Ursus [Euarctos] americanus.

83. Tamiasciurus douglasii
84. 1. Sciurus carolinensis
    2. Sciurus griseus
85. 1. Sciurus aberti kaibabensis
    2. Sciurus aberti aberti
86. Sciurus niger
87. 1. Glaucomys volans
    2. Glaucomys sabrinus
88. 1. Thomomys bottae
    2. Geomys bursarius
    3. Pappogeomys castanops
89. 1. Microdipodops pallidus
    2. M. megacephalus
90. 1. Perognathus hispidus
    2. Perognathus apache
91. 1. Perognathus formosus
    2. Perognathus parvus
    3. Perognathus intermedius
92. 1. Dipodomys ordii
    2. Dipodomys spectabilis
93. 1. Dipodomys merriami
    2. Dipodomys deserti
94. Castor canadensis
95. Onychomys leucogaster
96. 1. Reithrodontomys megalotis
    2. Reithrodontomys humulis
97. 1. Ochrotomys nuttalli
    2. Peromyscus eremicus
98. 1. Peromyscus leucopus
    2. Peromyscus maniculatus
99. Oryzomys palustris
100. 1. Neotoma lepida
    2. Neotoma albigula
101. 1. Neotoma cinerea
    2. Neotoma floridana
102. Sigmodon hispidus
103. Synaptomys cooperi
104. 1. Clethrionomys gapperi
    2. Microtus pennsylvanicus
    3. Microtus montanus
    4. Microtus californicus
105. 1. Lagurus curtatus
    2. Microtus longicaudus
    3. Microtus ochrogaster
    4. Microtus [Pitymys] pinetorum
106. Microtus chrotorrhinus
107. 1. Dicrostonyx torquatus
    2. Lemmus sibiricus
108. 1. Phenacomys longicaudus
    2. Phenacomys intermedius
109. Neofiber alleni
110. Ondatra zibethicus
111. Aplodontia rufa
112. Rattus norvegicus
113. 1. Mus musculus
    2. Rattus rattus
114. 1. Zapus princeps
    2. Zapus hudsonius
    3. Napaeozapus insignis

115. Erethizon dorsatum
116. Myocastor coypus
118. Lepus americanus
119. Lepus capensis [europaeus]
120. Lepus townsendii
121. 1. Lepus alleni
    2. Lepus californicus
122. Sylvilagus floridanus
123. 1. Sylvilagus audubonii
    2. Sylvilagus bachmani
    3. Sylvilagus floridanus
124. 1. Sylvilagus aquaticus
    2. Sylvilagus palustris
125. Sylvilagus [Brachylagus] idahoensis
126. Ochotona princeps
128. 1. Bison bison
    2. Ovis canadensis
    3. Antilocapra americana
    4. Alces alces
    5. Rangifer tarandus
129. Dicotyles tajacu
130. Odocoileus hemionus columbianus
131. 1. Odocoileus hemionus
    2. Odocoileus virginianus
    3. Odocoileus hemionus hemionus
    4. Odocoileus hemionus columbianus
132. Odocoileus virginianus virginianus
133. 1. Odocoileus virginianus virginianus
    2. Odocoileus virginianus clavium
134. Bison bison
136. Cervus elaphus
137. Alces alces [americana]
138. Rangifer tarandus
139. Oreamnos americanus
140. Ovis canadensis
141. Antilocapra americana
142. Dasypus novemcinctus
143. Trichechus manatus
144. 1. Balaena glacialis
    2. Physeter catodon
146. 1. Megaptera novaeangliae
    2. Balaenoptera borealis
    3. Balaena glacialis
147. 1. Sibbaldus musculus
    2. Balaenoptera physalus
    3. Eschrichtius gibbosus
148. Physeter catodon
149. 1. Micropteron mirus
    2. Hyperoodon ampullatus
    3. Ziphius cavirostris
150. 1. Phocoenoides dalli
    2. Phocoena phocoena
151. Globicephala sieboldii [scammonii]
152. Orcinus orca
153. 1. Delphinus delphis
    2. Tursiops truncatus [nesarnack]
    3. Stenella plagiodon

INDEX

An asterisk (*) designates pages on which subjects are illustrated; **bold type** denotes pages containing more extensive information.

MEASURING SCALE (IN MILLIMETERS AND CENTIMETERS)

MEASURING SCALE (IN INCHES)